Careers without College

Makeup Artist

by Kathryn A. Quinlan

Consultant:

Angela Nogaro
Makeup Artist
International Alliance of Theatrical Stage Employees,
Moving Picture Technicians, Artists and Allied Crafts of
the United States and Canada, Local 706

CAPSTONE
HIGH/LOW BOOKS
an imprint of Capstone Press
Mankato, Minnesota

Capstone High/Low Books are published by Capstone Press
818 North Willow Street • Mankato, Minnesota 56001
http://www.capstone-press.com

Library of Congress Cataloging-in-Publication Data
Quinlan, Kathryn A.
    Makeup artist/Kathryn A. Quinlan.
    p. cm.—(Careers without college)
    Includes bibliographical references and index.
    Summary: Describes the work of a makeup artist, including the education and
training required, duties, salary, employment opportunities, and possible future
positions.
    ISBN 0-7368-0175-8
    1. Theatrical makeup—Vocational guidance—Juvenile literature. 2. Film
makeup—Vocational guidance—Juvenile literature. [1. Makeup artists. 2. Vocational
guidance.] I. Title. II. Series: Careers without college (Mankato, Minn.)
PN2068.Q56 1999
792'.027'023—dc21
                                                                    98-45187
                                                                        CIP
                                                                         AC

Editorial Credits
Leah Pockrandt, editor; Steve Christensen, cover designer;
    Kimberly Danger and Sheri Gosewisch, photo researchers
Photo Credits
Anchorage Daily News/Steven Nowers, 30
David Falconer, 20
Leslie O'Shaughnessy, cover, 6, 18
Mary E. Messenger, 28
Photo Network, 4, 11, 38
Photophile, 9, 33
Rainbow/Dan McCoy, 12, 14, 40
Richard B. Levine, 16, 22
The Picture Cube, 36; The Picture Cube/Dede Hatch, 24
Viterbo College/Jennifer Bucheit, 26, 34

Table of Contents

Fast Facts 5

Chapter 1   Job Responsibilities 7

Chapter 2   What the Job Is Like 15

Chapter 3   Training. 25

Chapter 4   Salary and Job Outlook. 31

Chapter 5   Where the Job Can Lead 37

Words to Know 42

To Learn More 44

Useful Addresses 46

Internet Sites 47

Index 48

Fast Facts

Career Title_____Makeup artist

Minimum Educational_____U.S.: high school diploma
Requirement   Canada: high school diploma

Certification Requirement_____U.S.: varies by state
                                          Canada: varies by province

Salary Range_____U.S.: $15,080 to $95,000
(U.S. Bureau of Labor Statistics, Human   Canada: $12,100 to $53,600
Resources Development Canada, and other   (Canadian dollars)
sources, late 1990s figures)

Job Outlook_____U.S.: average growth
(U.S. Bureau of Labor Statistics and   Canada: stable
Human Resources Development
Canada, late 1990s projections)

DOT Cluster_____Service occupations
(Dictionary of Occupational Titles)

DOT Number_____333.071-010

GOE Number_____01.06.02
(Guide for Occupational Exploration)

NOC_____No code available
(National Occupational Classification—Canada)

5

Chapter 1

Job Responsibilities

Makeup artists are part of the field of cosmetology (koz-meh-TA-luh-jee). This broad field also includes cosmetologists (koz-meh-TA-lah-jists) and estheticians (es-thuh-TI-shens).

Estheticians, cosmetologists, and makeup artists each have certain skills and training. Estheticians specialize in skin care and makeup application. Cosmetologists specialize in hair care and styling. They also are trained in hand and skin care, and basic makeup application. Makeup artists specialize in artistic and personalized makeup. They usually develop advanced methods of makeup application used in TV, film, theater, and photography.

Makeup artists may specialize in artistic and personalized makeup.

Makeup artists use makeup to alter the bodies and faces of actors and models. They can make people look beautiful, scary, or older. Makeup artists can hide flaws and wrinkles. They also can create them.

On the Job

Makeup artists work in many different areas. These areas include film, TV, theater, as well as fashion and print advertising. Makeup artists use their skills differently for each area. But most makeup artists learn many of the same techniques.

Makeup artists usually apply makeup in layers. First they apply base. This creamy makeup gives a uniform color to faces. It also covers up flaws.

Makeup artists then use highlighting and shading. Highlighting is blending a lighter base to make an area more noticeable. Shading is blending a darker base to make an area less noticeable. For example, a makeup artist might use light-colored makeup to bring out a person's cheekbones. The makeup artist then might use dark-colored makeup to make the person's face look thinner. Makeup artists might add color by applying lipstick, blush, and eye shadow.

Makeup artists use highlighting to make areas more noticeable.

Makeup artists choose different makeup for individual faces and situations. A makeup artist might use a lighter base if an actor has delicate skin. Heavy base could cause an actor's skin to break out with blemishes. The makeup artist might use a long-lasting makeup if an actor has oily skin.

Film and TV

Makeup artists use their skills in many ways. For some shows they try to make actors, TV show hosts, and guests look as pleasing as possible. Sometimes they make people look like they are not wearing makeup.

Makeup artists may add special features to people. For example, they may add wounds or scars. Some of these features are created with makeup. Sometimes makeup artists create other parts to be added to people. For example, a makeup artist may create a fake nose or extra finger for an actor. These man-made items are called prosthetics. Makeup artists use their skills to make prosthetics look like parts of actors' bodies. Some makeup artists specialize in this kind of work.

Studios can take days, weeks, or months to film movies and TV shows. Makeup artists must pay attention to how actors need to look as scenes change. Makeup artists may need to make actors look the same throughout filming. But they also may need to show changes. For example, makeup artists might

Makeup artists apply makeup to actors for films, TV shows and programs.

make wounds appear to heal. They may need to show how characters age.

Makeup artists usually make models look appealing for print advertisements and fashion shows.

Theater Work

Makeup artists who work at theaters use special methods to apply makeup to stage actors. Film and television actors appear in close-up camera shots. Their makeup needs to look natural. But stage actors perform in front of audiences. They work under bright lights. The lights can make their faces appear pale. Makeup artists in theaters use heavy makeup. The makeup makes the actors' eyes, cheekbones, and lips stand out. Makeup artists try to make actors' faces visible to people sitting in the back row.

Fashion and Print Advertising

Makeup artists help prepare models for print advertisements and fashion shows. They usually try to make models look appealing.

Print advertising usually uses still photography. Models pose for photographers in still photography. Photographers often take well-lit, close-up photos of models for print advertising. Makeup artists in print advertising usually do not use heavy makeup. They want models to look natural.

Makeup artists in the fashion business prepare models for fashion shows and print advertising photos. The makeup for fashion shows is often heavier and brighter than makeup for print advertising. A dramatic effect often is wanted for fashion shows. Heavy, bright makeup gives this effect.

Chapter 2

What the Job Is Like

Makeup artists work with many different businesses. Their job experiences and work conditions depend on where they work. Most makeup artists work on a freelance basis. Companies hire freelance makeup artists for projects. TV and film studios also employ freelance makeup artists.

TV Work

Makeup artists who work for TV studios must be able to work flexible schedules. They need to be available whenever TV studios tape movies or programs. TV studios often tape programs during all hours of the day. For example, they often tape talk shows during daytime working hours. But other TV

Makeup artists work on different makeup projects.

TV makeup artists may work with many guest stars.

programs also may be taped during early mornings or late evenings. Makeup artists for these programs may have to work 12 to 14 hours in one day.

TV makeup artists usually work in specially built rooms at TV studios. These rooms provide the proper working surfaces, lighting, seating, and storage areas.

Makeup artists also may work on episodic TV shows. Studios film a new show each week for episodic TV shows. Some shows are filmed on location. This means the actors and filming crew travel to different locations. Makeup artists work in special trailers on location. This allows them to be mobile.

Makeup artists for episodic shows are hired for a show's season. A show's season can last nine months.

Makeup artists for situation comedies usually work two to three days each week. These half-hour comedy TV shows are sometimes called sitcoms. Makeup artists for sitcoms usually work in studios.

Makeup artists on TV shows may work with the same cast members each day. But they also may work with many guest stars. Makeup artists who work on talk and variety shows also may work on different guests each day.

Makeup artists often work in rooms at studios or in specially built trailers.

Makeup artists also may be hired to work on TV commercials. Companies film commercials inside studios or on location.

Film Work

Makeup artists who work on movies have the greatest variety of hours and duties. Studios film movies at all hours of the day. They film at many different locations. Movie makeup artists often travel to filming locations. The makeup artists may spend months working on locations far from home. They also may work nights and on weekends.

Movie makeup artists work in a variety of places. They may do most of their work in trailers. But makeup artists also must be available to touch up actors' makeup during filming on the sets. Makeup may become smudged and need to be fixed.

Makeup artists for films often spend many hours waiting to work. They may work a few hours to apply makeup to actors. Then for several hours they may have no work to do.

Special effects makeup can take hours to apply. Makeup artists who specialize in special effects often arrive many hours before filming begins.

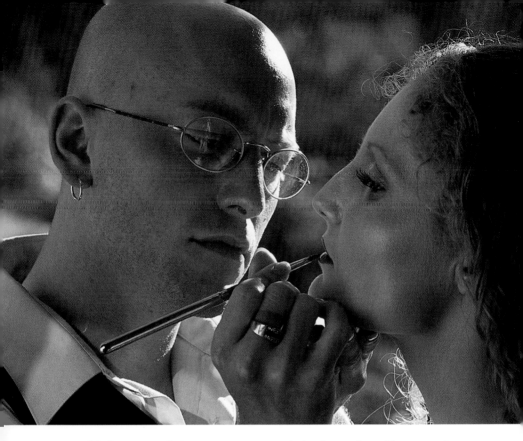

Makeup artists prepare models for advertisements and fashion shows.

Theater Work

Work times vary for makeup artists at theaters. The work hours for these makeup artists depend on show times. Makeup artists must be able to

20

prepare actors before and during performances. They also must reapply the actors' makeup between scenes and during breaks. They must be able to work quickly.

Theater makeup artists have a variety of duties. Makeup artists work with many actors. They may apply makeup to actors. They may style the hair of actors or make wigs. They also may give makeup advice to actors.

Fashion and Print Advertising

Makeup artists usually work freelance for fashion shows and print work. Advertising makeup artists sometimes work on location. For example, they may travel to a different state or another country. But they usually work in specially built studios. Makeup artists who work with print advertising and fashion shows may work steady hours.

Print advertisements often focus on models' faces. The advertising companies and photographers usually want models' makeup to be applied with

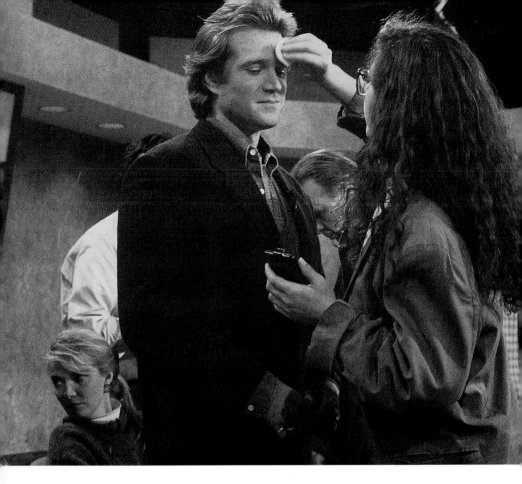

Makeup artists work with a variety of personalities.

great care. The companies and photographers may tell makeup artists exactly how they want the makeup to look.

Personal Qualities

All makeup artists share one challenge. They all work with a variety of personalities. Actors and models are concerned about how they look. Makeup artists often receive pressure to do what actors and models want. Some of these people can be difficult to please.

Makeup artists must work well with people. They must be able to help people feel comfortable and relaxed. Actors and models may feel nervous or under pressure when they work. It is easier for makeup artists to work when actors and models are relaxed.

Makeup artists need to be flexible. They must be willing to work unusual hours in unusual settings. Makeup artists also must be willing to travel far from home. They must be able to wait patiently for hours at a time to work.

Chapter 3

Training

There are no minimum educational requirements for makeup artists in the United States or Canada. But most employers require makeup artists to have completed high school. Most makeup artists train on the job.

Makeup artists advance slowly as they gain experience. They often begin by assisting experienced makeup artists. Makeup artists also may start out working at community theaters or small TV stations. Some gain experience by serving as apprentices. These makeup artists work with master makeup artists for several years. Some apprentices even pay to work with skilled makeup artists. But this is not a common practice. It takes about five years of work and training for an apprentice to become a skilled makeup artist.

Makeup artists gain experience in many ways.

Students can learn how to apply makeup in classes.

Many makeup artists seek formal training in their field. They study in programs designed for makeup artists at universities or cosmetology schools. Other makeup artists study theater arts at four-year community colleges or universities.

What Makeup Artists Study

Makeup artistry students take a variety of classes. They take classes in how to apply makeup. Students also study how to create special effects makeup. Many students learn how to cut and style hair. Makeup artists may work on both hair and makeup on some jobs. Students also study how to make wigs. Makeup artists may create wigs for theater actors.

Students may take courses in health and chemistry. Health courses teach students how to avoid spreading germs when working with makeup. Chemistry courses teach students about chemicals and other ingredients used in making makeup and prosthetics.

Some makeup artistry students study theater arts. These students may learn about makeup and costumes. They also may study set design, lighting, and direction.

Other subjects also are useful to makeup artists. These include drawing, painting, and sculpting. Makeup artists are like other artists in many ways. They must understand how colors and shapes work together. They use their makeup brushes and pencils to create a variety of effects.

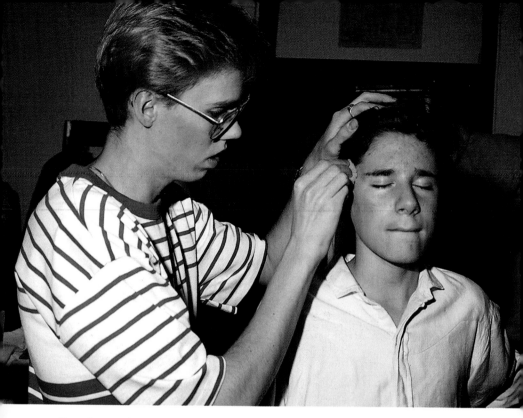

Students interested in makeup artistry can do makeup for school plays.

Students may take communication classes. Makeup artists must communicate well with actors and models about their makeup needs. Makeup artists also must communicate with directors and other studio people about how they want actors to look.

Licensing

Makeup artists may need a license to show and apply makeup. Some states and provinces require people to have cosmetology or other special licenses. People may have to complete training at a school and take a test to get a license. Each state and province has different requirements to get a license.

What Students Can Do Now

Students interested in makeup artistry can gain experience in several ways. They can offer to do makeup for school plays. They can take courses in makeup from local schools or community education programs. They can do face painting at local events. Students can read trade magazines to learn more about makeup artistry. These magazines are publications for people in a certain business.

Students may talk with makeup artists. They can ask makeup artists about the field and how to enter it. Students who want to talk with makeup artists can contact schools, theaters, or TV stations.

Students also may be able to work part-time in cosmetic departments at local stores. These students can learn about makeup by helping people choose it.

Chapter 4

Salary and Job Outlook

Makeup artists in the United States earn between $15,080 and $95,000 per year (all figures late 1990s). Makeup artists who earn higher wages usually work steadily all year long. The average annual salary is about $55,040. The low end is based on a group average by the U.S. Bureau of Labor Statistics. This group also includes barbers and cosmetologists. The high end is from other sources in the makeup artistry field.

Makeup artists in Canada earn between $12,100 and $53,600. The average annual salary for makeup artists in Canada is about $32,600.

Makeup artists' salaries vary with their experience and skills.

Makeup artists who belong to a union can earn higher wages. For example, an union makeup artist in Hollywood can make up to $95,000 per year.

Most makeup artists belong to unions. These groups help makeup artists negotiate salaries. To negotiate means to discuss something until two or more sides reach an agreement. Unions work with theaters and studios to establish base salaries. Base salaries are the lowest salaries makeup artists can be paid for certain jobs. But experienced makeup artists usually earn more money.

Most makeup artists work on a freelance basis. They are paid for individual projects. They may not have steady work. Makeup artists may work for three or four months on one project. They then may have two months without work or income.

Successful makeup artists can count on regular work. They also can charge higher rates than other makeup artists. Makeup artists who belong to unions also usually make higher incomes than other makeup artists. But some makeup artists must find ways to add to their incomes. Some makeup artists take non-union makeup jobs. These jobs have lower salaries than union jobs.

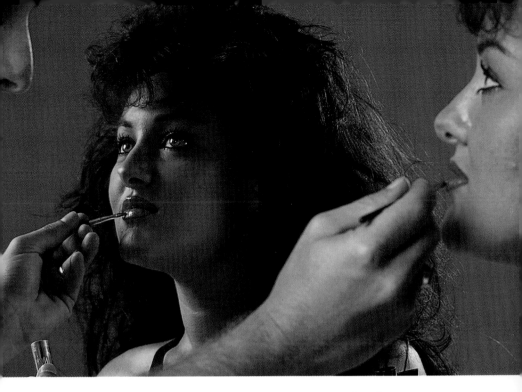

Most makeup artists work on a freelance basis.

Some freelance makeup artists work with agencies that help them find jobs. Print and fashion work makeup artists mainly use agencies.

Benefits

Makeup artists who have full-time jobs usually receive benefits from their employers. Benefits may

Makeup artists work in entertainment businesses.

include paid vacations, health insurance, and retirement plans.

Makeup artists who belong to a union may get insurance free or at lower group rates. Union makeup artists also can contribute to retirement plans. These plans save money for makeup artists. Union makeup artists use this money after they retire.

Job Outlook

Makeup artists mainly work in entertainment businesses. Their job prospects depend a great deal on the economy. People spend more money on entertainment when the economy is doing well. Film studios make a profit and produce more films. Theaters put on more plays. Makeup artists then have more opportunities for work.

Makeup artistry in the United States is expected to have average growth in the future. The outlook for all makeup artists in Canada looks fair through the year 2001.

Makeup artists have many job opportunities. The number of TV, cable TV, and other media programs grows each year. Makeup artists also can work with companies that make computer-generated programs. They can do the makeup on the individuals in the programs. These shows can be viewed on computers.

Where the Job Can Lead

Makeup artists advance as they gain experience. Some makeup artists may become well known through their work. Makeup artists who are known in the entertainment and advertising businesses often have many chances for work. They also can earn more money. Some makeup artists become well known by winning awards. These makeup artists often can choose their jobs. They also receive much higher salaries than other makeup artists.

Advancement

Freelance makeup artists may advance by finding full-time jobs. Makeup artists in some areas may

It can take hours to apply makeup for some shows.

Makeup artists sometimes must do both hair and makeup for a show or program.

advance by becoming managers. Managing makeup artists oversee other makeup artists.

Union makeup artists who want to become managers must take a union test. The union test is very difficult. Managers receive higher pay than other makeup artists.

Makeup artists also may advance by getting jobs that pay higher salaries. For example, theater makeup artists may advance by finding jobs in TV. Makeup artists who work on TV shows may advance by finding work on movies. But salaries are not only based on where makeup artists work. For example, not all TV makeup artists make more money than theater makeup artists.

Not all makeup artists want to change where they work to advance. Some makeup artists prefer to work with theater. Others like to work on films. Makeup artists advance when they work on the programs and shows they like.

Other Opportunities

Makeup artistry is a challenging profession. It is not a career in which everyone succeeds. Many people try to enter the business each year.

Many people interested in makeup artistry do not become makeup artists. They may enter a related career. Some of these people apply makeup at a salon or department store. Those who work at cosmetic counters focus on selling products rather

than applying makeup. Some people also sell makeup through home shows. Others become image consultants. These people help others improve their appearances.

The Future

Makeup artists always will be needed in the film and TV industries. They also will be needed in the theater, advertising, and fashion industries. There are many jobs for makeup artists when these businesses are doing well.

Makeup artists stay successful by constant research and study. They also must be skilled in their jobs. Makeup artistry is a highly challenging and rewarding profession. Makeup artists can become known for their abilities. Endurance and talent are necessary to be successful in the field of makeup artistry.

Makeup artists often can use their creativity when they apply makeup.

Words to Know

agency (AY-juhn-see)—a business that provides a service to the public

apprentice (uh-PREN-tiss)—a person who learns a craft by working with someone skilled in that area

cosmetology (koz-meh-TA-luh-jee)—the science of treating the skin, hair, and nails

estheticians (es-thuh-TI-shens)—people who are trained in hand and skin care, and the use of cosmetics

freelance (FREE-lanss)—to be paid for each job instead of by the hour or through a yearly salary

makeup (MAKE-uhp)—products used to color or enhance the face or other parts of the body

negotiate (ni-GOH-shee-ate)—to discuss something until two or more groups come to an agreement; a union negotiates pay rates for some makeup artists.

prosthetic (pross-THET-ic)—an artificial part that alters a face or body; special effects makeup artists apply prosthetics such as scars and fake noses.

union (YOON-yuhn)—a group that seeks better treatment and fair pay for workers

To Learn More

Cosgrove, Holli, ed. *Career Discovery Encyclopedia.* Vol. 2. Chicago: J. G. Ferguson Publishing, 1997.

Delamar, Penny. *The Complete Make-up Artist: Working in Film, Television and Theatre.* Houndmills, Basingstoke, Hampshire, England: Macmillan Press, 1995.

Kehoe, Vincent J. R. *The Technique of the Professional Make-up Artist for Film, Television, and Stage.* Boston: Focal Press, 1995.

Lincoln, Margaret. *Face Painting.* The Most Excellent Book Of. Brookfield, Conn.: Copper Beach Books, 1997.

Swinfield, Rosemarie. *Stage Makeup Step-by-Step: The Complete Guide to Basic Makeup, Planning and Designing Makeup, Adding and Reducing Age, Ethnic Makeup, Special Effects.* Cincinnati, Ohio: Betterway Books, 1994.

Useful Addresses

International Alliance of Theatrical Stage Employees, Moving Picture Technicians, Artists and Allied Crafts of the United States and Canada (IATSE) Canadian Office
258 Adelaide Street East
Suite 403
Toronto, ON M5A 1N1
Canada

IATSE
1515 Broadway
Suite 601
New York, NY 10036

National Cosmetology Association
3510 Olive Street
St. Louis, MO 63017

Internet Sites

Human Resources Development Canada
http://www.hrdc-drhc.gc.ca/JobFutures/
  english/volume1/522/522.htm

IATSE
http://www.iatse.lm.com/

Makeup Effects by Lars Carlsson
http://www.makeup-fx.com/Indexeng.html

Occupational Outlook Handbook
http://stats.bls.gov/oco/ocos169.htm

Stage Directions
http://www.stage-directions.com

Index

advancement, 25, 37–39
advertising, 8, 13, 21, 37, 41
agencies, 33
apprentice, 25

benefits, 33-35

cosmetology, 7, 26, 29

education, 25, 29
estheticians, 7

fashion, 8, 13, 21, 33, 41
film, 19 *See also* movies.
freelance, 15, 21, 32, 33, 37

license, 29

managers, 38
movies, 10, 15, 19, 39 *See also* film.

prosthetics, 10, 27

salary, 31–32
skills, 7, 8, 10
special effects, 19, 27

theater, 7, 8, 12, 20, 21, 25, 26, 27, 29, 32, 35, 39, 41
training, 7, 25, 26, 29

union, 32, 34, 38